TIPS

Technology for Music Educators

Compiled by
Charles G. Boody

Music Educators National Conference

T0303429

ISBN 0-940796-72-4

Table of Contents

Foreword

The Music Educators National Conference (MENC) has created the TIPS series to provide music educators with a variety of ideas on a wide range of practical subjects. Each TIPS booklet is a compilation of methods, ideas, and suggestions that have been successful in the music classroom. MENC has designed this quick-reference series to be used as a starting point for creating and adapting projects for your particular situation.

TIPS: Technology for Music Educators is designed for music teachers at all levels who would like some new ideas about how best to implement some of the newest tools available to the profession.

Introduction

This little book is organized around the topics of the materials contributed. I have attempted to collect materials that speak to similar matters but have not limited contributions through some *a priori* overall design. The table of contents should be sufficient guide for those looking for specific topics. In the interests of completeness, I have added an appendix: it is a brief and selected list of further resources. In the interests of keeping the resources in the appendix reasonably current, I have largely ignored books and kept it limited to what a librarian would call occasional periodicals and directories or sources of information that are updated at least yearly. The appendix would best be viewed as a "bibliography of bibliographies" or a guide to sources.

Readers should not perceive this book as taking a cookbook approach to using technology, nor should they expect to find all (or even most) of their questions answered here. What they will find are useful "how to" hints, caveats to new users, and the distillation of many useful generalities. The information should excite and support those making first steps in using technology and provide food for thought for those with some experience in the field. Contributors to this book come from universities, colleges, public schools, and private teaching. Their perspectives and perceptions differ, but they share some important traits: an enthusiasm for the new technologies, experience in using them in their own situations, and a willingness to share what they have learned. Throughout the book readers will sense the excitement of the contributors for the new wind blowing in our profession.

Foremost among the difficulties in producing this book has been the word "technology." The word should limit the domain of the book, but it is a term that is largely defined by the context in which it is used. A dictionary of some twenty years ago gives the study of the industrial and practical arts as its first definition of technology. In that broad sense, musicians have always been great users of technology. Musical instruments, from the humble song flute and Autoharp to gigantic pipe organs, are miracles of technology, and the complex (and sometimes absurd) system of notation we use is the product of centuries of tradition and development.

In more recent years, the now-common technology of recorded sound has allowed us to greatly change the way we teach music. As recently as the 1940s the only efficient way to study music was through study of scores—a practice that in turn depended on developing ability to analyze those scores without the benefit of hearing them performed. First, recorded performances became available to the music teacher and student. Later, recording technology allowed us to listen critically to our own attempts at producing music and thus improve our skills. To today's music educators, if one judges from the contributors to this book, the word technology means mostly computers and electronic keyboards of various sorts. This is appropriate, for those technologies are completely changing the ways people create, produce, and consume music. The same advances in technology that made those devices possible, however, are also producing other new devices: compact disks, video disks, high-definition television, constantly more efficient and more powerful computers, communications networks, specialized devices for producing music or modifying musical sounds, programs and machines for automatic transcription of musical performances, and digital audio tape recorders. Because of these continual developments in the field, some of the tips included in this book may be obsolescent soon after it is published. To preclude that possibility as much as possible, I have avoided most references to particular machines or programs. Concepts that technology allows us to use, and the sometimes hidden pitfalls in using them, are and will remain important.

Specific makes and models of equipment are sometimes listed in this book: these references are an attempt to clarify information about the resources necessary for each teaching idea. Mention in this book is not meant as an endorsement by MENC or its affiliates.

Implicit in most of the tips are these important generalizations:

- The new technologies provide tremendously expanded tools that students can use to become actively involved in creating music and communicating in musical ways. It is as though we have moved abruptly from drawing with charcoal on rocks to drawing with the whole spectrum of colors on a canvas that can be stretched to whatever proportions we desire.
- The advent of devices that allow the user to access materials randomly greatly simplifies the study of music. In under a second, one can locate and access any point on a compact disk—and the location can be accurate to 1/75 of a second. In a similar manner, video disks can be accessed in less than 2 seconds to show an individual frame, or to find the starting point of an example. The starting point can be accurate to 1/30 of a second. Finally, the sounds and pictures produced by these devices do not degenerate with repeated use.
- The rapidly falling cost of electronic keyboards with powerful capabilities seems to have reasserted the importance of offering keyboard experiences for students. Such instruments could replace the Autoharp, recorder, and Orff instruments by providing the same types of musical learnings with tools that can do much more.

- Any attempt to use new technologies requires more effort than ignoring them will require. Students grasp new things more easily than teachers, because they are familiar with the new devices and because those devices produce sounds to which they relate.
- The use of new technologies can help school music overcome accusations that it is irrelevant to today's students. This is not an argument for ignoring the classics or for avoiding the teaching of musical skills. Rather, it is a recognition that many students will be more interested in musical elements or techniques (chords, for example) when the sounds produced are relevant to the music with which they are most familiar. In a similar way, the use of video-based materials can reach today's more visually oriented students better than posters or recordings.

All of these points imply that it is once again time for music teachers to struggle with questions regarding what to teach and how to teach it. In the past, curriculum was often defined by circumstance rather than by what should be taught. Our first music performance groups were vocal, partly, at least, for the reason that we could always sing without any additional materials at all. Pianos became a staple in the classroom because they provided the most flexible and cost-effective tool for accompaniment and teaching. Now we have a huge number of ways to approach music, but the circumstance-controlled curricula of the past have been in place for so long that we may not easily see that tradition rather than rational thought is the basis for much of what and how we teach music. Many of these new ways are relatively inexpensive, but we continue to approach teaching using methods that do not take advantage of the rich possibilities we now have.

We live in an exciting age for music teachers. Technical advances are providing new and varied tools for the music performer and teacher, and the growing interest in traditional and ethnic musics makes today's students more willing than those of a generation ago to listen to and perform a great variety of music. Perhaps this book can help teachers deal with one of the many exciting things that are happening.—*Charles G. Boody*

Technology's Role

The Microcomputer as a Carrier for Arts Education

Everywhere one looks—in schools, businesses, around the community, and in the local newspaper—one sees examples of the latest wave of word processing, now promoted to the title of desktop publishing. A similar revolution is going on in music and graphics, so desktop publishing has become desktop arts production. With low-cost microcomputers we have desktop presentation graphics, desktop composing and arranging, and desktop animation. With software now available, you can quickly produce professional-looking overheads or, if you wish, a completely interactive video presentation directly from a microcomputer.

Using the new industry standard, Music Instrument Digital Interface (known as MIDI in the industry), you can connect an incredible palette of drum machines, keyboards, and instrumental sound generators to a microcomputer and then coordinate your own desktop orchestra with any of the several software packages designed to facilitate composing and arranging. Just as desktop publishing has hundreds of fonts to choose from, desktop composing has libraries with hundreds of music instrument sounds ranging from a conservative grand piano to an exotic Japanese *koto*. If your piano keyboard skill is of the hunt-and-peck variety, "sequencer" software lets you enter the music in layers: the melody, the harmony, the percussion track, and other parts can be handled separately. If you can't keep up with the tempo, you can enter the music at your own pace and then have the computer execute the *prestissimo* performance. With software such as MicroMinds VideoWorks II, you can choreograph a completely animated music and graphics event.

As arts educators, we have a wonderful opportunity through this technology to promote arts education, music education, and aesthetic education beyond the traditional school environment. There is one critical set of elements that computer hardware and software does not provide: the artist's eye, ear, and hands. The technology simply provides the tools, albeit powerful ones. There is little to no artistic or aesthetic sense built into the desktop software: the choices of color, font, text style, harmonic content, shape of melodic line, rhythmic contrast, and other style variables are all artistic decisions. On the one hand, this points out the greater need for training and experiences in the arts to complement and enhance one's computer skills. On the other hand, this also requires teaching a sensitivity to knowing when a professional artist's input on graphics and music production becomes critical to the aesthetic impact of a finished product. *(Portions originally published in the Bloomington, Illinois,* Pantagraph, *November, 1989)*—DBW

Implications for Teacher Education

- Future music educators can be prepared to use music technology in their own teaching by the integration of computing and music technology across the college music curriculum.
- College music education students who learn music theory with the help of computer-assisted instruction for aural skills can use the same procedures with their high school music theory classes.
- In orchestration and arranging classes, assignments can include creating scores for specific instrumentations that are typical of elementary and secondary school performing groups.
- Piano classes can incorporate new, functional piano skills that include operating electronic keyboards and synthesizers and playing arrangements created for school ensembles.
- Methods instructors can build on the use of computing and music technology across the college curriculum by addressing issues such as the integration of music technology into public school curricula, lesson planning to incorporate creative uses of music technology, instructional uses of electronic keyboards and synthesizers, selection of appropriate hardware and software, strategies appropriate to different learning styles and skill levels, the use of music technology to promote higher-level thinking skills, and possibilities offered by this technology for self-expression by students with disabilities.—JB

Music Theory Instruction

For a long time, computers have been used for computer-based instruction (CBI) in the areas of music theory and ear training. The principal CBI mode has been drill-and-practice—the computer has proved to be very effective for that purpose. With the advent of the MIDI standard (which allows many instruments and computers to share information) and very fine notation software packages, however, the computer can serve as a composition and arranging tool that may even surpass the effectiveness of CBI for music instruction. For example, rather than drilling students on the spelling and identification of triads, it might be far more productive to give students a composition assignment in which they are asked to play chords of various qualities on a MIDI keyboard, arpeggiating and voicing the chords in various ways. Connect a computer to the keyboard and use sequencer software, allowing the students to store their triad-based compositions and play the music back, experimenting with different timbres—using the keyboard and computer for a much more creative learning experience than the drill-and-practice mode affords. Use the same software to set up ear-training exercises and ask the students to play chords that will harmonize with melodies that are stored on diskettes, recording their solutions on the same diskettes, which you can hear and grade later.—MA

* * *

Musical elements and harmonic concepts could and should be taught with a keyboard and a set of headphones for each student at every class. As a topic is discussed, give each student opportunities to play chords and their resolutions, intervals, modes, melodic lines, step progressions, and so forth. Students should receive as much immediate aural reinforcement as desired and learn through a tactile dimension.

We traditionally encourage students to use a keyboard after class (or institute a required keyboard harmony class to insist that they do so). The best kind of keyboard learning, however, is that which occurs at the time of the written presentation. The best kind of keyboard for this learning is a synthesizer with the capacity for a number of different timbral colors, which ensures that the theory doesn't seem to pertain to piano music alone. And portable keyboards, which could be tucked under the arm after class is over, are useful tools in the student's home or dorm. They can be used for composing, arranging, or just completing written assignments, thereby reducing the number of mystified expressions when the instructor asks, Do you know what this sounds like? The versatility, quality, and low cost of portable synthesizers are making this scenario possible. It should go without saying, however, that this classroom format may require different teaching skills than the traditional approach.—KC

* * *

Synthesizer technology and existing music composition and printing programs can embellish and strengthen the teaching of counterpoint. Have students enter their work with an alphanumeric (typewriter) keyboard or a synthesizer keyboard, hear the composition with the tempi and timbres they desire, and then print their work. Editing the piece is not difficult. Students who find it difficult to hear four-voice counterpoint internally can now learn to judge their exercises aurally as well as visually—and the teacher's bonus is an assignment in neat, legible notation.—KC

* * *

We may be reaching the time when theory assignments that are not printed by computer in good-quality notation are as unacceptable as handwritten themes would be to an English teacher.—CGB from TK

Computers and Computer Software

Getting Started

Don't simply ask "What kind of computer should I buy?" That question approaches the problem from the wrong direction. You need to think of a computer not as a piece of hardware to plug in (like a toaster) but as a component in a complete system. This system has five equally important parts: people, procedures, data, software, and hardware. The "people" in this case are those who are going to use this computer system: music students, teachers, performer/composers, administrators, or a combination of these. "Procedures" means how the computer system is to be used: for music instruction, performance, or composition; marching band charting; production of newsletters, programs, and sheet music; in inventories of equipment, uniforms, records, and sheet music; or to handle traditional administrative tasks such as typing, budgets, scheduling, mailing lists, and the like. "Data" is what the computer system is going to process or transform (that is what a computer is after all, an electronic device that transforms information): numbers, text, music notation, music sounds, user responses (from a unit such as a keyboard, an instrument controller, or a drum machine), and graphic images. "Software" is the set of instructions that enables the computer to perform a task. You need to investigate what computer programs are available, either commercially or in the public domain, that will meet the needs of your particular combination of *people, procedures,* and *data.* Only after these investigations do you get to the last question: "What computer hardware should I buy?" Given your assessment of the people, procedures, data, and software, you can easily pick the best hardware or computer equipment.

You will be amazed at how much more helpful a salesperson in a computer store can be if you walk in with this information in hand. There are a variety of microcomputers of different types suitable for different educational and musical tasks and different student populations. Decide what you want to do with a computer, and *then* go shopping.—DBW

* * *

Consult your computer center staff or educational computer consultant for information on relevant journals, professional organizations, special interest groups, conferences, and meetings. Discuss your aims with colleagues who are using music technology and can provide advice on introducing computing and music technology into your program.—JB

* * *

Do not reinvent the wheel. Seek out national and local support groups and publications. Locate a music store near you that offers music software. Research your school or campus computing culture to discover the type of hardware that is used, what machines would be available for your use, whether you would have access to a computer lab, whether a computer could be located in your classroom, and so on. If your school already owns a number of computers, you may be limited to software that is compatible with that hardware. If not, examine the software first and then determine your hardware needs.—JB; TR

* * *

Become an active member of professional educational and computing organizations. National, division, and state meetings of the Music Educators National Conference, the Music Teachers National Association, and The College Music Society regularly feature a number of beginning through advanced sessions on computing and music technology. Several Special Interest Groups (SIGs) relevant to music technology exist within the Association for the Development of Computer-Based Instructional Systems (ADCIS). These include SIG/Music, also known as the Association for Technology in Music Instruction (ATMI) and SIG/IVA for Interactive Video-Audio. General sessions are helpful in understanding broad issues related to educational computing. The Small Computers in the Arts Network (SCAN) features sessions in music, film, video, graphics design, animation, sculpture, and multimedia. These organizations provide a forum for discussion among people interested in computing in education and the arts.—JB

* * *

Read software reviews in professional journals to discover what software is available for the areas in which you are interested, where you can obtain it, and how others are using it. The various MENC state journals regularly feature software review columns. Journals that address educational computing and the professional musician such as *Electronic Learning* and *Electronic Musician* are also good sources for reviews. You will find occasional music software reviews in commercial computing magazines (both general publications and those specific to a particular type of computer).

From these sources, select programs you wish to secure for further review. Read the articles on educational computing and music technology that are frequently found in these journals for ideas on implementing your program. Determine whether use of a keyboard will enhance your approach, and, if appropriate, select software that includes a MIDI option.—JB; TR

* * *

When you obtain the software you have selected, follow a systematic review process that will allow you to compare the programs you have chosen. Review a cross section of educational software appropriate to the level you wish to work with (for example, young children, elementary, and so forth).—JB

* * *

Have a friend or colleague help you load and run some software that is of interest to you. If your friend is a novice, you will get a better idea of how the student may react. If you are the novice, you will get that same information and will become more experienced yourself.—EB

* * *

Attend a workshop on computers and music. Summer workshops are listed each spring in the *Music Educators Journal* and other places. This is the best way to become aware of the new technologies that were not available while most of us were attending school.—TR; EB

* * *

Identify your needs that can be met by the computer (such as keeping track of student data, music, uniforms, grades, and assignments; producing music arrangements; writing letters; producing programs or publicity materials; or almost anything else). Your need to solve administrative problems will motivate you much more than some sort of vague feeling that you ought to know something about this, and overcoming these administrative problems will help you become familiar with the computer. Once familiar, you will be much more comfortable using the computer with students, and your awareness of the computer's uses will expand.—BJ; TR

* * *

- Plan time and money for all three facets of using technology: hardware purchase, software purchase, and staff training. The last factor is usually ignored and should be carefully considered.
- Integrate technology with your existing curriculum. Use it with your performing groups and music classes before worrying about a "Computer and Music" elective.
- Try to do unique things with the computer, such as composing, arranging, and printing music. Try to avoid using the computer as a page turner. Ask yourself the question, "Can this be done as efficiently without the aid of the technology?" If the answer is "yes," then by all means do it without the technology. If the answer is "no," then you have found a good use.

- Consider connecting an electronic keyboard to a computer via a MIDI interface (a device that allows the computer to communicate with MIDI-capable instruments). This will open up a new world of MIDI software.
- Do not fool yourself into thinking that technology will be the panacea for music education. It will not. It can, however, become an exciting tool for your students use and yours.
- Plan for the long term; purchase equipment that will last. Sometimes this means buying things that are not the least expensive items available. Cost is important, but longevity is vital.—TR

* * *

The successful implementation of any new method, material, or technology depends on careful planning and appropriate preparation. Here are eight steps that outline one plan for integrating microcomputers into an existing music program:

1. Get training in computer basics. Do some reading to familiarize yourself with the vocabulary of computing. If the make or model of computer that you will be using is a given, get the training on that specific hardware.
2. Review your administrative tasks to see where you might want to use computers to help.
3. Review your curriculum to see where technology might help you, and decide what kind of software might be helpful. To some degree this step might be concurrent with step four.
4. Evaluate the software available in terms of subject content, instructional format, vocabulary, and clarity of instructions and explanations. (This evaluation might be carried out concurrently with the preceding step.) Based on this evaluation, select the software you intend to use.
5. If possible, base your hardware selection on the software you want to use. If this is not possible because your hardware has already been chosen, look at software for the appropriate machine—but keep your eyes open! There may be a piece of software that will justify the purchase of a special computer. Once the hardware is available, be sure that it is situated so that it is available to all students, including those who are physically impaired.
6. Code your software in some way that describes it. You might use classifications by *group size* (LG=large group, SG=small group, I=individual use); *instructional level* (A=advanced, R= remedial, S=supplemental), and *instructional format* (DP=drill and practice, EC=exploratory/creative, SM=simulation, T= tutorial). List your software, indicating the appropriate codes and providing each item with a separate number (try *CPG #*; the let-

ters stand for "computer program number"), and use that identifying number in your curriculum units and lesson plans.

7. Plan to get further training on setting up the system, working with MIDI, and other such matters. Be sure you are aware of your local support people for this training; there may be more help available than you think.
8. Continue to examine new software that can expand your possibilities. This sounds time-consuming and tedious, but many teachers have found the administrative and instructional results worth the effort.—GT

Teaching and Administrative Uses

Every music educator should develop competence with the three most common types of general applications software: word processing, database, and spreadsheet programs. Once mastered, these programs can be used for many of the administrative tasks that every teacher must perform. Several integrated programs are available which combine these applications (and often others as well) into one package. Specific names include Appleworks (for the Apple II or Apple IIGS), Microsoft Works (for the Macintosh and IBM or compatible), and Desk-Mate (Tandy IBM-compatibles). While the individual applications in such packages are usually not as powerful as stand-alone programs of the same types, they are quite sufficient for beginning- and intermediate-level users. Furthermore, the various applications in these packages are easier to learn than the same applications purchased separately, because they share many keystroke commands and have a common user interface.—JKW

* * *

Many people who use word-processing software seem to know little about the wonderful tool called the spreadsheet. Spreadsheets, such as *VISICALC* (the first such program), can carry out the obvious numeric tasks: spreadsheets are wonderful for budgets (great for playing with the numbers to find a best fit for those meager music education funds); grading (how could you better answer the question, "What grade do I need on this exam to pass the course?" than dynamically show a student the effect of a hypothetical grade on a final grade); and any sort of accounting (from simple tallying of fund-raising receipts to a complete system for all of your funds). There are also some not so obvious uses of spreadsheets: A spreadsheet can be used as a database to store mailing lists, student information, music instrument repair data, information on sheet music and recordings, and many other things. Most spreadsheet programs have features for sorting, finding, reformatting, and selectively printing information.

The designers of the newer generation of spreadsheets have capitalized on this concept and have strengthened the database features of their programs. Think of a spreadsheet as a large sheet of paper with rows and columns marked off across the computer screen—and the addition of computer intelligence so that the sheet becomes dynamic. Anything you can imagine putting into this form with pencil and paper can be done on a spreadsheet—including computing a matrix of row forms for a 12-tone piece! Do you hate setting up tabs for tables in a word processor as much as I do? Use the spreadsheet to do the formatting for you; set up your rows and columns, enter the data into the spreadsheet, and then export the chart from the spreadsheet to the word processor (most spreadsheets and word processors have already worked out this exchange, so it should be very easy to implement). When you export the spreadsheet, it brings all its tabs with it, so when it appears in the word processor everything is nicely formatted. Make friends with your spreadsheet and enjoy!—DBW; JKW

* * *

Database programs can be used to file and retrieve information on practically anything: a library of choral music, a collection of recordings, or an inventory of school-owned instruments, uniforms, or robes. I would not recommend purchasing a specific-purpose filing program for these tasks. Such programs usually embody someone else's conception of the problem and its solution; you will no doubt have (or want to develop) your own solutions to the demands of your own situation. Although a general-purpose database program may require a greater initial investment of time and mental effort to learn, it will ultimately prove to be much more flexible and valuable than special-purpose software.

I would also not recommend undertaking a large filing project until you are thoroughly familiar with the basic concepts and techniques of database management. Spend the first several hours learning your program and setting up small database files and report-generating formats in order to acquire a sense of what is possible. Then, when you feel ready to tackle a big project, think carefully about the categories that you will require, the nature of the data within each category, and the types of display and report formats that you will need. In the process of doing so, you will be surprised at how much you learn about your data and the various possibilities for organizing it. Remember that decisions about database structure and report formats are usually not irrevocable. Any good program will allow you to make changes after the data-entry stage has begun. Nevertheless, an initial period of careful thought and a few trial runs with a representative subset of the data can often enable you to avoid revision.—JKW

* * *

The huge administrative load faced by music teachers, particularly elementary school teachers, can be appreciably lightened by using a computerized record-keeping system to track student progress. In larger districts, district-wide catalogs of music can save funds by helping teachers avoid duplicating purchases of music that is already on hand. Remember, though, to honor copyright requirements—if enough schools share current works, the published music supply will disappear.—CGB

* * *

Put uniform records and instrument inventory on databases. This makes sign-out procedures and updating very easy.—CW

General Computer Tips

Save everything you create on data disks. At the end of a year, or the beginning of a new year, you will have lots of completed and useful materials, and you can quickly and easily adapt or redo those materials that were not successful.—EB

* * *

Do become aware of the five types of music software: Drill and Practice, Tutorial, Music Games, Composing/Printing Software, and Testing Software. Each is applicable in different circumstances.—TR

* * *

Although numerous programs that display and print standard musical notation are now available, I would encourage music teachers at every level not to overlook the educational potential of programs that use alternative schemes for representing music. Remember that our traditional system of notation has evolved over several centuries and is primarily intended to facilitate performance. When music is studied from other perspectives (such as listening, analysis, composition), other systems of representation may be more appropriate. Working with such alternate schemes can often enhance one's understanding of aspects of the music that are obscured by traditional notation—and are often, therefore, taken for granted. Also, investigate the potential of computer programs that provide an environment for "learning by doing." They may be more difficult to learn and less focused than programs that are designed to drill or teach a specific task, but such programs can provide rich learning experiences for student and teacher alike.—JKW

* * *

We are often given to conceiving of programs we would like to see, programs that would plug neatly into our curricula and would be mind openers for our students. At the outset, however, it is impossible to grasp the enormity of the task. One must have an in-depth understanding of a programming language and its machine-dependent characteristics, as well as a knowledge of program design, program flow, and user interface. And writing programs always takes much longer than expected. Any programming project should be approached with fear and trepidation. If a program that would be suitable in any way is available on the market, purchase it and use it (with thanks to the author or authors who gave so much of their time to its creation). If you persist with the folly of software design, you should make an early decision as to whether you are writing the software for your particular situation only or whether you hope to market it. If you hope to sell the program you may wish to seek the advice of publishing companies as you are completing the program's design and before you have begun the actual work of programming. A decision to develop a commercial product may necessitate the inclusion or exclusion of certain features. For example, many commercial courseware programs include the capability for scoring and grade-keeping of students' results. Also, vendors may be unwilling to sell a program because of the choice of language or the use of special items like overlays for the computer keyboard. Early planning and a willingness to compromise on certain aspects of your work will ease the frustrations of adapting to the commercial market, but may also water down your wonderful idea.—KC

* * *

Copyright and Software: You owe it to yourself to respect the copyrights on all computer software. The music industry, through ASCAP and BMI, has spent years educating the profession and the public about the important effect of copyright on music creativity; the same concepts and ethics apply to computer software. Here is a nonlegal summary: Most manufacturers allow users to make one archival copy of software that you purchase. That means you can make a backup of your software in case you should damage the original. It does not mean that you can then loan your backup to a fellow music educator or make multiple copies for your students to use on multiple machines or buy one copy for your school district.

The next time you buy a new software package, stop and read the fine print before you break open the shrink-wrapping: the legal restrictions may frighten you. Most companies, for example, operate on the one-machine-only concept, which means that you purchase this software to be used on one machine only. In addition to the important ethical considerations, matters of economic common sense apply here. If you want the few software companies producing quality music education software to stay in business and the authors to keep writing new and innovative software, respect the copyright laws. Thanks.—DBW

* * *

Choose your own application level for using computers. The fear of using computers in music education is not as prevalent today as it was ten years ago, but many educators are still reluctant to "dive in" and experiment with computer technology. Many educators have the impression that being "computer literate" means knowing how to write computer programs, but nothing could be further from the truth. An analog to swimming-pool psychology might help explain the difference among these levels. Based on our experience with water, we select the low end of the pool (where we are only wet up to the waist or wading), the middle of the pool (where we can still touch bottom if we need to), and the deep end of the pool, which the high divers inhabit. Satisfaction is attainable at all three depths. The last thing a sane wader would do is to head for the diving board; similarly, a beginning computer user should never start by programming a computer. He or she should pick the appropriate level of wading (buy-and-run), and work his or her way up to swimming with the bottom in reach (fill-your-own), and finally if desired, to high-diving (roll-your-own).

Buy-and-run applications are those for which you need only know how to insert the computer disk and turn on the machine (just about as easy as using a video tape recorder, and substantially easier than threading film in a projector). Hundreds of such software applications are available for all kinds of microcomputers. Programs can be found for music fundamentals, ear training, music history/literature, music analysis, and as elements of series designed to accompany textbooks or aid in instrumental skill development and many other subject matters. All of these are computer applications that you simply buy, put in the computer, and run. In fact, the most challenging part of this level comes from what you have been trained to do best: to match the large variety of computer software to your music curriculum.

Fill-your-own applications are those that do not have specific working content. That is, someone has programmed the logic of the computer software's functioning but left it void of content so you can fill in content that is tailored to your needs. This level of computer application requires more skill than the buy-and-run one because you need to learn enough about the particular fill-your-own application to add your music content. Fill-your-own software falls into three categories: administrative, instructional, and creative. There is an incredible array of software available in each of these groups that will meet most needs for users of almost any computer. In the administrative category, we have word processors, spreadsheets, database programs, grading and scheduling programs, various music inventory software, and the like. In the instructional category are programs that let you build instructional materials by typing in the content of the questions and the possible correct answers. Software developed with the latest generation of hypertext-based packages provides the best combination of flexibility and ease of use for instructional software designed at a fill-your-own level. In the creative category is software that lets you design graphics, newsletters, and posters; compose and notate music; design marching-band charts; and produce a host of other products that come from manipulating computer-generated sound and graphics.

Roll-your-own applications are the "12-foot-depth" level of expertise. Here you need to get down to the nuts-and-bolts level (although this may be with varying degrees of expertise) and learn how to design and write your own software. At this level you must learn a programming language (from BASIC or FORTRAN to PASCAL or C, one of the more immediately accessible authoring languages like LOGO or PILOT, or one of the newer multimedia language implementations of hypertext such as *HyperCard*, *HyperStudio*, *LinkWay*, or *OmniCard*). With the significant variety of buy-and-run and fill-your-own applications accessible to music educators, few educators will want to concern themselves with roll-your-own applications.—DBW

* * *

LOGO is a medium for expressing powerful ideas. It is especially good for representing and processing data that are grouped or hierarchically structured. Much of the data that we musicians process in the act of studying or performing music has these characteristics. Most versions of LOGO have some capability for playing music, but that capability is often severely limited in terms of sound production. Certain LOGO dialects, however, offer more extensive support for musical sound generation. Terrapin Music LOGO for the Apple II (produced by Terrapin, Inc.) and Object LOGO for the Macintosh (produced by the Apple Programmers and Developers Association) are two such versions.

What are some of the powerful ideas that a student of music might explore using a musical version of LOGO? You might begin by investigating musical forms and processes. How do smaller units (motives and phrases) combine to form larger units (periods, groups, and sections)? What is the proper balance between retained and changed elements in a variation? What are some of the principles that govern imitation in a motet or fugue? What would it sound like if the same piece were played using a different scale? How does the structure of music resemble that of language? As some of the above questions imply, LOGO can serve as a tool which enables the investigation of relationships among various artistic domains.

LOGO is based on the philosophy of Piagetian discovery learning. Students learn about music by designing networks of short programs (called procedures), which collectively create musical objects or solve musical problems. Because LOGO is an extendable computer language, environments can be designed to meet the student at his or her level of expertise. For example, you can use it to convince students who have had no formal musical training that they already have an intuitive understanding of musical structure and style. It can also be used to help competent performers develop their musical cognitive abilities more fully.

One major difference between LOGO and traditional computer-aided instruction is that LOGO programs typically do not judge a student's work. The responsibility of deciding whether a program accomplished its intended task is left up to the student and his or her peers. The teacher's task in designing or selecting LOGO activities is to place the student in a context where he or she can successfully discover what the teacher wants learned and to offer occasional suggestions when students get stuck or discouraged.—JKW

Software Selection

Be sure you buy software that is made for the brand of computer that you are using. Know the specifications of your computer—especially its memory capacity—and its software limitations. Also be sure to read about what other equipment is needed to run a piece of software. It may require a mouse, digital entry pad, game paddles, joystick, MIDI interface, or a special sound board.—JC

* * *

Be careful with rhythm training software. Some of it demands an unreasonable level of tapping accuracy by the respondent; other programs are much too forgiving. Look for software that has variable thresholds for error, so that you can adjust the program's sensitivity to match the student's ability and the computer's capability.—PA; CGB

* * *

Preview software before purchasing. Software is like sheet music: You must review it in order to select the most appropriate piece.—TR

* * *

When reviewing software, "be" your students. Examine the program from the students' point of view. Are attractive graphics used? Is there a minimum of text on the screen? Is a good deal of interactivity used? How many incorrect answers are allowed before the correct one is given? Can the student escape? Are several difficulty levels available so the student can gain a sense of progress and accomplishment? Is on-screen help available? Is typing skill necessary? Are few keys required for response entry? Make the kinds of mistakes students make: press the wrong key or enter an outrageous answer and observe how the program responds. Were these situations anticipated and provided for by the designers?

If you are examining the software from the teacher's point of view, ask these questions: Are there several levels of difficulty that will extend the usefulness of the program over a broad range of students? What portion of your course will the program cover? Regarding ease of use: Are clear and complete on-screen instructions included? Is the number of keys required for response kept to a minimum? Is a help list available? Is on-screen text presentation minimized and interactivity maximized? Regarding user control: Can the student select exactly the materials he or she wishes (for example, only major and minor seconds and thirds)? How much flexibility is allowed in the selection of materials? Does the program move on automatically or after the user presses an appropriate key such as Return? Regarding error correction: How many attempted responses are allowed? Are specifics regarding the type of error noted in the error correction (such as "Too low, check the clef" in a notation drill)? Are comparisons between incorrect and correct responses given? Regarding record keeping and teacher utilities: Are records kept on disk? Can the teacher alter the content (for example, by specifying groups of intervals to be presented at certain levels or by entering melodies to be played)? Regarding sound: How is sound generated? Will you need any peripheral equipment? Is the program available in a MIDI version? Is the program one that does not use sound, such as a program that deals only with the identification of terms?—JB

* * *

Begin on a small scale. Select one area of your curriculum that might be better approached with the use of music technology, such as note reading. Design a simple syllabus that will coordinate course content and software (such as tutorials, drill and practice, and games). Organize the materials in sequence by difficulty level. Implement your plan with a small number of students in an experimental class, giving each participating student a copy of the syllabus.—JB

* * *

Track each student's progress. If your software includes record-keeping routines, you can print out scores for each student. You might keep an index card file or a database of tasks assigned and completed; students then can check off assignments as they complete them, or computer lab assistants can help update the records. Compare achievement of students with different learning styles. Evaluate attitude as well as learning. Note which programs are most effective and which ones the students like best.—JB; EB; BJ

* * *

Computers are a great motivational tool for the practice of music fundamentals. There is a variety of software available for most of this subject, and using this software appears to speed up the learning process for the students.—EB

* * *

Games make drill enjoyable: students focus *on* the game and *off* the difficulty of the task. Games may be a preferred approach: they are interesting from the start, so students stay on task longer.
Games are intrinsically motivating: they offer a challenge, sometimes by means of timed drills. Uncertainty generated by random selection of questions engages the curiosity. Finally, in some games, the element of fantasy can be a powerful motivator.—JB

* * *

I once had a student who, when told to work on software that drilled intervals, wanted a good score—so she chose one hundred problems that used only perfect fourths. Of course she had a perfect score, but she fooled herself: the perfect fourths appeared all over the staff and she really learned to recognize them because of all the repetitions.
There are two implications here: First, software may allow the students ways around your instructions (particularly if you do not understand the software well enough to be specific in your requests). Second, learning may take place in some very unexpected ways, particularly with new technologies, and we need to be alert to take advantage of these new approaches.—PA

Electronic Keyboards and MIDI

MIDI (Musical Instrument Digital Interface) is an international standard that allows keyboards, drum machines, personal computers, and an array of new music equipment to communicate music in a common language. MIDI standardizes the electronic details of how signals should be sent and received and also standardizes the meaning of the signals sent. For example, pressing middle C on a MIDI keyboard will send information that a key was depressed, the number 60 indicating middle C, and a number indicating the speed with which the key was depressed. This standardization allows many different kinds of electronic musical equipment to work together.

In practice, MIDI simply means that instruments can be connected to and from a system (using MIDI in and out connections) by a five-prong cable, which plugs into the back of the instrument. MIDI is as important to electronic music as standardization of phonograph speed, cassette recording speed, and compact disk sampling speed have been to the recorded music industry. Without it, each keyboard would have its own methods of communication, and each computer program would be limited to those devices for which the programmer had provided. This standardization means that teachers can develop a set of electronic equipment that can interact, and that you can add to or update your equipment rather than replace everything (as was common before MIDI).

Despite the standardization that has been achieved, there are still many options available to manufacturers—options that can cause the user difficulties. For example, MIDI allows devices to transmit or receive on any of 16 channels, but some devices will only send or receive on specific channels. Some keyboards with built-in drum patterns and chord patterns will not transmit those patterns. Other keyboards will transmit drums on one channel, a bass line on another, chords (vamps) on a third, and melody lines on a fourth or fifth, but will not allow the user to choose the channel for each item. If you have two devices that both transmit only on channel one, you will not be able to use them simultaneously without problems. If you have two devices that will receive on only one channel, you will not be able to transmit selectively to one of them without shutting off the power to the other. There are solutions to this sort of problem in the form of MIDI channel changers and other such devices, but they cost money and time. The novice buyer may purchase an item that requires such extra devices if he or she is not aware of the issues.

Do some reading about MIDI before becoming involved with electronic musical instruments and associated music software. Your local library may be of help, and if not, the sources listed in the Appendix to this book provide a good start. There are several books with the theme "MIDI for Musicians" that explain the details of MIDI systems very clearly.—CGB; BJ

Selecting an Electronic Keyboard

Selecting your first electronic keyboard can be difficult, to say the least. Having struggled through this process of trying to select a keyboard and being frustrated by "techy" talk, I finally decided to identify the features to consider before selecting an instrument. Once I had identified the features I wanted, I had fewer keyboards to select from and the choice was much more manageable. Here is a list of the main features you might consider when purchasing your electronic keyboard:

The manual: The first step is to page through the keyboard manual and see if it seems readable and understandable. If so, that is an excellent sign that you're on the right track. Most manuals will list the keyboard's features along with general operation information. I like to check to see which MIDI channels a keyboard will use to send and receive information. For example, if you are going to connect your keyboard to a computer for drill and practice, your keyboard must send and receive on channel one, because most drill and practice software uses that channel. In the back of the keyboard's manual there will be a MIDI implementation chart or MIDI specification chart. An excellent way to test your dealer is to ask for the keyboard's MIDI implementation chart. Most dealers will know where that information is found and how to decipher it. If your question brings panic to the eyes of your dealer, it may give you an indication that the dealer has little knowledge of the equipment to be sold.

Multitimbral: The multitimbral feature is my top priority, because I use my keyboards to record parts and create accompaniments. The ability to use the different timbres in parts can be fun and bring real life to the simplest of accompaniments. The multitimbral question is usually answered under the MIDI section in the manual. The manual will tell you how many timbres (preset tones) may be played (accessed) simultaneously and how many notes (polyphony) each timbre will play. Ability to assign MIDI channels to individual preset or custom-designed timbres gives the keyboard the multitimbral capability. In the MIDI system, each channel may be assigned only one voice or preset tone, so if the keyboard has three channels available, three voices can be accessed simultaneously. The multitimbral feature of a MIDI keyboard is used primarily when the keyboard is connected to a sequencer. (A sequencer is a recording device, usually a computer, that saves the MIDI information.) Most major keyboard companies now have multitimbral keyboards available. These keyboards are priced as low as $200.

Built-in speakers: The inclusion of built-in speakers connotes an inexpensive home-entertainment keyboard. My first two MIDI keyboards needed separate amplification. This is fine if you have that amplification handy. As I began to experiment with keyboard/computer stations, however, extra amplification for each keyboard began to be a real headache. I now see built-in speakers as a real asset, and I consider them a must for a student keyboard.

Ins, outs, and thrus: Of course, we are talking about a MIDI keyboard. You will need a MIDI "in" connection and a MIDI "out" connection (both of which are present on almost all MIDI keyboards, though it is possible to find a few MIDI keyboards with only a MIDI out connection). A MIDI "thru" connection (along with MIDI in and out ports) is useful if you are electronically chaining your keyboards together. Devices called "MIDI thru boxes" will give you the same feature, so don't eliminate the keyboard if it does not have a thru port.

Headphone jack: The "phone out" connection allows you to connect a headset to the keyboard. This feature is a must in keyboard labs. The "line out" connection of a less expensive keyboard will also work just fine for a headset. I prefer the MINI line out of the inexpensive keyboards because inexpensive, stereo headsets will plug right into them. (For the most part, these are stereo units.) The more expensive keyboards have quarter-inch jacks and will need an adaptor if you are using inexpensive mini phone plug headsets.

Sustain pedal: A sustain pedal, connected to the "sustain out" port of the keyboard, will allow the notes played to be held even after the keys of the keyboard are released (just like the sustain pedal on a piano). This feature can add considerable user control. I am starting to use a sustain pedal much more than I did in the past.

Volume pedal: I think this feature adds musical flexibility to the keyboard, and it can be found on less-expensive MIDI keyboards. Pedals are a great addition, especially to a non–touch sensitive keyboard (on which you cannot control volume by varying the pressure of your fingers on the keys).

Automatic accompaniments and separate volume controls: Volume controls allow you to adjust the volume of your accompaniment (chordal, bass, or percussion) independently of your melody. On some of the new inexpensive keyboards I have found that these volume controls are connected to separate MIDI channels, allowing dynamic adjustments of individual parts or use of just the bass line or automatic rhythm. This is a major improvement and is very useful in creating accompaniments. The ability to receive and send MIDI clock information, which allows you to synchronize one instrument's part with another, is crucial to the usefulness of your auto rhythms and auto accompaniments. The auto accompaniments on some of the newer keyboards are far more flexible than the old "boom-chuck," unvarying accompaniments most of us remember hearing on home organs. They now respond to different inversions of chords in different ways, have variations and beginnings and endings in various styles, and can play just drums, just keyboard vamps, or just sustained chords. Some keyboards have additional programmed patterns available to expand the flexibility of the accompaniments.

Velocity sensing (key velocity): This feature is what distinguished the piano from the organ; it provides control according to the initial speed of the key stroke. Pianists will want velocity sensing for it gives them greater expressive control. This feature was a high priority for me, primarily because it provided a way to control the relative volume of parts of different timbres. With some of the less expensive new keyboards that do not sense velocity, however, you can control the output volumes of separate MIDI channels, which may give you the needed control without velocity sensing.

Keyboard split: The ability to split a keyboard is often confused with the multitimbral feature of some keyboards. A keyboard split is more limited, but it may be used in live performance and multitimbral techniques cannot. The split allows you to play two or more sounds at the same time, assigning each to a different area of the keyboard. For example, if there is one keyboard split, the lower notes may play a string bass sound while the upper notes play a piano sound for the melody. Some expensive keyboards allow you to split many times, assigning many different timbres. The most obvious use for this feature is that of a number of "single key splits" that allow the performer to play percussion sounds while playing melodies on most of the instrument.

Key transpose: The transposition function allows you to alter the pitch of the keyboard up or down by half steps. For example, while you play in the key of C, the keyboard can produce notes that sound like you are playing in the key of B. This makes it very easy to change accompaniments to match the key that your students need. I have found that some keyboards transpose only by moving up from concert A=440 or down from concert A=440, and others transpose up or down 5 or 6 half steps. In the past, key transposition was very important to me. Because I now often save my accompaniments to a computer disk, I can transpose as needed from the computer that controls my keyboard. With this technique, I don't need to remember what key I transposed to.

Tuning control: As the new breeds of inexpensive MIDI keyboards are created, I'm afraid that some manufacturer may see fit to leave this feature out. It is important in a combo setting, or even in a lab setting where students playing together need the ability to tune their keyboards. Theoretically, all of the keyboards are at A=440, but other instruments may not be, and pitch standards change.

The sound: Too often, in my opinion, keyboards are selected for their sounds only, with very little consideration given to features and the flexibility of future use. The sounds of a keyboard are usually called "voices" or "preset tones." The amplifier system used with a keyboard makes a major difference in how that keyboard will sound. Often amplified systems have ways of altering the quality of a keyboard's voices. Also, you will be amazed at how good the least expensive keyboard will sound through a good amplifying system. It might be worth your time to ask for the keyboard on approval so you can hear it with your own sound system. The more expensive MIDI keyboards are programmable, which is useful but not much used, because the process of programming new sounds can be rather complex. The presence of programmability usually means that the user can easily save sounds and add new sound banks to a keyboard. Adding new sounds can also be done by adding separate sound modules which are often much less expensive than a MIDI keyboard of the same quality.—BJ; CGB

Using Automated Keyboards

- Use automated keyboards (those that have automated bass and rhythm patterns) with or in place of an Autoharp or when teaching the I, IV, and V7 chords.

- Students can learn to improvise easily if given a simple rhythm and a simple chord progression from a familiar song.
- Have students play a given melody with I and V7 chords and have others improvise on the chords to create harmony parts.
- Sharpen listening skills by creating exercises using the various timbres available.
- Use single-finger-bass chord patterns when teaching rounds.—JC

* * *

- Some keyboards and sound modules will allow you to send your tracks in stereo. This allows you, for example, to use the left channel for alto and the right channel for soprano by placing the speakers in the correct position to support the singers. Some of the keyboards allow you to create your own accompaniment in duple or triple meter.
- Try experimenting with students teaching students. To do this, you can link all of your students together via headsets in a "mini keyboard" teaching lab.—BJ

Combining Electronic Keyboards and Computers

Getting Started

When you connect your MIDI keyboard to a personal computer via a MIDI interface, the real excitement begins. Your computer becomes, through the use of sequencing software and your MIDI keyboard, a recording studio. Using your MIDI recording studio you can record one part on top of another part and save your work on a floppy disk. Later you may want to change your work's tempo, key, melody, or harmonic structure. This can be easily done through the many edit capabilities that sequencing software contains.

I use my computer and MIDI keyboard primarily for classroom accompaniments. With my guidance, sixth graders have used this recording process to create original works for a musical play they wrote. Part singing can also be supported by sequencing software, especially if your MIDI keyboard has stereo outputs and ability to send one part to the left channel and one part to the right.

Warning: If you have never used a computer, sequencing software may not be the place to start. My suggestion is to start using a computer for word processing, keeping a database, or for simpler stand-alone music software, so you can become more familiar with how a computer works before tackling sequencing software.

To begin you will need:

- *A personal computer*. An Apple II+ or other inexpensive castoff may work just fine. Remember, this computer is easy to come by in most public schools because it doesn't run some of the newer word processing software.
- *A MIDI keyboard*. Selecting a MIDI keyboard can be very difficult if it is your first keyboard. I suggest that you begin with a less expensive keyboard and use it to explore the ways that you might use MIDI. My first MIDI keyboard cost $300; a multitimbral keyboard is now available for $200.
- *A MIDI interface*. A MIDI interface connects the computer to the keyboard and has two cables connected to its in and out ports. There are a number of companies that make MIDI interfaces for personal computers. Make sure that the interface you are purchasing is *Passport* compatible if you intend to use Apple II series software from more than one company. You must do this because the MIDI interface used in most Apple IIe products has been the

internal (*Passport* compatible) interface. This interface card fits into slot 2 inside the computer. It will interface with any Apple II series computer. Two MIDI cables (in and out) connect to the interface card, pass through the back panel of the computer, and connect to the MIDI keyboard. It has been important for the Apple IIgs users to run the IIe MIDI software with the internal interface to allow access to the large collection of drill and practice MIDI software for the IIe. When the Apple IIgs was released, provision was made for using an external MIDI interface. The external interface is a small box that has MIDI in and MIDI out ports where the two MIDI cables are connected. The other end of the box has a serial cable (the type that connects to the modem or printer port on the back of the Apple IIgs). This external interface can be interchanged with either the Apple IIgs, or the Macintosh line of computers.

The MIDI programming tools for the external MIDI interface were not ready, however, when the Apple IIgs was released. Software developers have been making Apple IIgs MIDI products that are, for the most part, able to run on either internal or internal and external interfaces, but that is gradually changing as more and more developers provide for only one or the other. Until recently it was possible to use all of the instructional MIDI IIgs software with the internal interface. I now believe, however, that for the future (certainly for the near future) you will need an external and internal interface if you want access to all MIDI software for the Apple IIgs and IIe machines on your IIgs. You will also need added memory on the older gs models in order to run much of the newer software.

- *MIDI cables.* Cables are usually included when you purchase your interface, but not always. You will need at least two.
- *MIDI software.* I suggest that you begin with a user-friendly, less-expensive sequencing package.—BJ

Synthesizers, Sequencers, and Notation Programs

The stand-alone sequencers are just now starting to drop in cost and may be very cost-effective for creating small composition stations at which students can work with a MIDI keyboard, creating their own compositions.—BJ

* * *

Create special parts for students with changing voices. As the students' needs change, you can easily edit and reprint the parts.—CGB

* * *

When there is not enough time to learn an accompaniment, you can enter the accompaniment one part at a time and play it back with all parts together.—EB

* * *

- By putting vocal and accompaniment parts on separate tracks, you can play just vocal parts, vocal parts and accompaniment, or just accompaniment as needed. In performance, the vocal parts can be sent to separate speakers (located where they can support the singers but are less easily heard by the audience).
- By recording the parts of a work on a sequencer and playing them back on multitimbral synthesizer, you have an entire "orchestra" available to accompany classroom work and performances.—BJ; EB

* * *

Because sequencers can be set to repeat a recorded tune "forever" (a process called looping), you can record a singing game ahead of time and then get out on the floor and work with the students. Starting and stopping the recording is managed with a single key press, and sequencers and synthesizers can be used to lower or raise the pitch level of the music or change the tempo (without changing the pitch). That way, the needs of the class can be much better met than with a recording. Also, your problems of discipline are reduced when you are not bound to the keyboard playing accompaniments.—CGB; BJ; EB

* * *

Take advantage of the editing features of composer/sequencer software to teach basic music concepts. Teach canon by entering a song such as "Three Blind Mice," copying and pasting to build the canon; use the transpose, retrograde, and other features of the software to build a fugue. Teach timbre by altering harmonic spectra to produce different tone colors. Teach basic concepts of rhythm by creating rhythm tracks that use steady beat, accent, offbeats, or syncopation. Illustrate ostinato by entering a pattern and setting a loop.—JB

* * *

Use a sequencer to build accompaniments. Then spice up your accompaniments with the built-in rhythm and chord patterns that are available on many keyboards.—BJ

* * *

- Enter the various voice parts of a choral composition in separate tracks. Play only those tracks, along with the accompaniment track, that you wish a class or group of students to learn. Use only the accompaniment track or tracks during the performance.
- Keyboard instruction is possible in a school setting with the proper software.
- Use sequenced material to provide an accompaniment while students play melody instruments such as recorders, bells, or guitar (melody only).
- Realize on a keyboard the part of an instrument needed to complete an ensemble.
- Record the "other partner" in a piano duet.—JC

* * *

By using the looping capability of most sequencers, ostinato accompaniments in the Orff style can quickly be created and used as a basis against which the class can improvise. Similar loops can be used to help teach jazz improvisation.—CGB

* * *

- When telling students the story "behind the music" of a work such as Sergey Prokofiev's *Peter and the Wolf*, use the synthesizer keyboard and "correct" timbres and themes to help prepare students for the actual orchestral composition listening experience. Students can understand the concept of "it sounds like..." very quickly.
- Have students create music with appropriate timbres for stories that can be used to teach concepts. For example, "Goldilocks and the Three Bears" can be used to illustrate high and low register.—JC

* * *

Students at the elementary level are able to begin composing their own music. A simple sequencer program that allows students to enter notes and hear the results can lead to long discussions about why students made the musical choices they made. Be prepared, however, to hear lots of freely atonal and highly unstructured pieces!—EB

* * *

We, as teachers, want students to learn about form and structure, so we tend to try to "help" the students by fixing their compositions so that the result has a "better" structure. Be careful! This was not a problem when we didn't have a way to make the musical experience as immediate as it can be when we use the new technologies, but several times my "improvements" have caused students to burst into tears because I had tampered with their aesthetic ideas. Remember that your ideas aren't really better, they are just different—and there are only value judgments when one begins to deal with aesthetic issues.—BJ

Miscellaneous Equipment and Ideas

Large Monitors

For music teachers planning to use computers or video in their classroom, the first piece of equipment to consider is a large TV monitor. This device should be at least 25" size, and should be "high resolution." High-resolution units can produce more than 400 lines of resolution, and so can adequately reproduce the high-quality images of laser videodiscs. The unit should have several inputs for video signals, and if the unit is to be used for audio, it should have quality stereo sound capabilities.

Those planning to use computers with the monitor should also be sure that their computers can be easily hooked to the monitor. Usually, it is not necessary for a music teacher to buy such a unit, but he or she must be sure that one is available. If you plan to make heavy use of the unit, offer to "store" the unit in the music room so that it is easily available for classroom use. Once the unit is available, take care to place it so that students can easily see and hear. Consider such matters as distance from the screen, reflection of light off the screen, height of the screen, width of the room, and the like. (This seems very obvious, but is often overlooked.) The unit has many uses: besides being available for video materials it can serve as an electronic blackboard, as a station where computer-based materials can be used by the entire class, and as a means of introducing students to materials they will later use in a computer lab.—CGB; BJ; RJ

Graphics Programs

Use one of the powerful graphics programs that are available for any microcomputer. These programs allow colorful graphic displays and animations to be easily developed, and are part of the current push toward "desktop presentations." Because much music material (such as notation, piano keyboard, fingering charts, and rhythm patterns) is graphically based, such displays can be very useful in music class. Consider the possibility of a display that shows fingerings for a recorder on demand or one that shows notes on a staff simultaneously with a piano-style keyboard (as did the old electronic piano lab devices). Students love to work with graphics and are often willing to get involved in the design and production of the displays. Best of all, the displays can be saved and modified as teaching situations demand; this allows you to continue to adapt and develop the materials rather than to be tied to some particular set of pictures or displays.

If business executives see this as useful enough to their presentations so that they learn to use the tools, music educators can also use them.—BJ; CGB

Audio Mixers

Use an audio mixer in the music classroom to allow you to play more than one sound source at a time. There are a number of these mixers out now that will take up very little space and will enhance and simplify the use of MIDI sound sources, keyboards, tone modules, drum machines, CD players, computers, cassette players, and phonographs.—BJ

Drum Pads and Drum Machines

Use drum pads, assigning each to the control of a separate sound source, to duplicate the kinds of things that can be done with Orff instruments. One of the reasons Orff designed the instruments he did was to make available to students instruments of real musical quality and accurate pitch that can be used to produce real music with minimal technical skill. Electronic instruments have all of those characteristics. Sixteen MIDI playing devices (such as drum pads, electronic keyboards, or MIDI wind controllers) and one 16-channel sound source would allow lots of creativity of the sort that Orff envisioned.—BJ; CGB

* * *

Drum machines are made to create and store rhythm patterns. Many of them will hold twenty or more one-measure patterns and allow these short patterns to be combined and stored as several longer patterns. Often these patterns can be "dumped" to a computer through a MIDI connection and stored for easy recall at a later date. Use these capabilities to create one-measure rhythmic dictation exercises for students.

- Control the drum machine patterns as the entire class plays games like "rhythm bingo," or group students in teams and have one team quiz the other by selecting the rhythm patterns. Five correct in a row might give the winners the right to ask questions rather than answer them.
- Because drum machines can be set at any tempo, exercises using them can be easily adjusted to student requirements; and because the machines can easily be made to act as metronomes, students can hear patterns against a steady pulse if so desired. Once students are comfortable with one-measure patterns, use longer patterns for more extended exercises. Students will learn to hear patterns in rhythm this way rather than lengths of individual notes.

- Most drum machines can generate about sixteen sounds, and each sound can be assigned a MIDI key press number (the same number that would identify the pitch on a keyboard). One can then send the numbers to a MIDI sound source (almost any electronic keyboard will do). Each percussion part will then be played as a series of different pitches, making it much easier to hear the different parts of a complex rhythm. The availability of sixteen pitches and up to (usually) sixteen events within a measure makes it possible to use the drum machine as a small sequencer in creating melodic ear-training patterns. Because drum machines can make several different drums sound simultaneously, chord progressions can also be created using this same technique.
- Drum machine patterns can be very quickly and easily created, and sets of materials can be easily stored on computer disks. You can quickly develop libraries of materials for classroom and individual rhythmic, melodic, and harmonic ear training that can be adapted to the needs of students at any level. Those interested in more esoteric matters will discover that the graphic display of many drum machines can clearly show voice-leading and chord voicing for advanced students.—BJ; CGB

Laser Disc Technology (Videodisc and CD)

The laser disc formats available to the music instructor can be placed into two main categories, Laser Videodiscs (LV) and Compact Audiodiscs (CD). The LV discs are found in two sizes, 12" and 8" diameter. The videodiscs can be encoded on one side or both. They store the video information in two formats: the Standard Play (CAV) format offers access to any one of 54,000 individual frames and/or 30 minutes of video. The Extended Play (CLV) format can hold twice as much information on a single side, but it can only be accessed to the nearest minute and second. Unless an expensive player with special capabilities is used, you cannot view a still picture on a CLV disc.

The new Compact Disc-Video (CD-V) discs come in 4 3/4" discs as well as the 8" and 12" sizes. The 4 3/4" CD allows more than 70 minutes of digital audio to be recorded on one side of the disc; 3" CDs are also available. Three newer variations of the CD format are now beginning to become available. These are: Compact Disc+Graphics (CD+G), Compact Disc+MIDI (CD+M), and Compact Disc+Graphics+MIDI. These variations use the normal audio CD and add computer graphics information, MIDI information, or a combination of both into a special 30 megabytes of space on the disc. This information could be used to supplement the music on the disc. For example, the text of an art song can be shown on a television screen (in several languages) while the song is being performed. Similarly, encoded MIDI information on a CD could be retrieved and used to print scores of the music or provide a musical accompaniment for a soloist. The potential of this technology for education is exciting.—ES; LP

* * *

- CDs, like computer discs, are a random-access medium. You can, with the proper equipment, go directly to any location on a CD with an accuracy that is within 1/75 second. That is quite different from trying to find the second theme of the exposition of a major symphonic work on a record (*scraaaaatch*) or cassette ("Just a minute, it's near here, no that's not it, oh it's at 765.... I forgot to set the counter.... Oops, the counter on this machine is different from mine.... Well, tomorrow we'll have time to look at...."). Second, the sound will not deteriorate each time the CD is used, and starting in the middle will not cause any kind of wear. Third, some CD players have the ability to be programmed to play sections of a disc on command, and will remember the series that you want to play the next time you put the same disc into the player. Unfortunately, most of those programmable players are only programmable by track and not to 1/75 second, so the buyer must be sure what he or she is purchasing.

  Finally, and most exciting, there are implications in the newer CD formats. Computer interface also adds exciting possibilities. Users can, with simple "point and click" interfaces, select exactly what bits and pieces of a disc they want to hear and store the list on the computer—or develop simple point and click games or guided listening exercises for students (without the need to program the games).
- Laser Videodiscs address an important characteristic of many of today's young people: their orientation to visual presentations, cultivated by their many hours of viewing television. Also, some musical forms (opera, ballet, and Broadway musicals are the obvious examples) can only be properly appreciated when the visual aspect of the works is present. Students respond enthusiastically to opera instruction and admit that their opinions when they entered the course—thinking of opera as elitist, boring, or old-fashioned—have changed to enjoyment and appreciation. Finally, LV can bring rare instruments, rare performances, and world-class musicians into the classroom with video and digital audio sound of the highest quality. This makes the study of instrumental timbre and musical performance practice much more accessible.—ES; CGB; LP

* * *

Whether you are teaching general music in a public school or music appreciation in a college or university, sooner or later (usually sooner) you teach the elements of music: melody, texture, harmony, form, timbre, and rhythm. Laser technology is particularly useful in teaching concepts initially difficult to grasp, such as texture and form. Discs such as the *Bachdisc*, published by Voyager, and the discs in the University of Delaware Videodisc Music Series help with these problems because they provide visual clues to the texture and form through color-coded scores, colorful diagrams that move as the music is performed, and camera work that emphasizes the texture and form. Some of the commonly available videodiscs of performances have underlined form and texture through the choice of visuals shown as the music unfolds.—LP

* * *

There are two interesting and very different performances of Giacomo Puccini's *La Bohème* available on videodisc, and I recommend them as a starting point for teaching about opera. My experience has been that students are reluctant to talk about an opera, but if you show them two productions of the same opera and ask them to compare the productions (such aspects as lighting, acting, costumes, and singing), they will talk about the performances and the works at length. I see wet eyes among the students at the end of Bohème.—LP

* * *

I ask students to make a visual map or outline of a work of their choice using the guidelines in the common music appreciation texts. With CDs and computer interface, an interested student can actually present an aural analysis of a work from his or her own collection. This helps me learn what they are listening to and whether they can use the musical vocabulary we are trying to develop in class. It also stimulates the students to listen very carefully to observe the musical details of the performance. One can do this with records or tapes, but the easy access to any point on a CD without damage to the disc makes it much more possible.—LP

* * *

Current list prices for CDs range from $9.95 to $21.95 for a single disc release. Already, CDs have essentially replaced LP records. Prices should fall, since actual production costs are lower for a CD than for an LP. There are countless CDs available with almost every known musical style well represented. Folk and ethnic musics have lagged behind, but are beginning to be available. Most LV discs of musical performance cost between $25.95 and $69.95, though specially produced LVs for education may cost up to $1,000.00 each. Currently, at least twenty-five ballets, six choral works, one hundred jazz titles, eighty Broadway musical titles, seventy-five opera titles, seventy-five orchestral titles, twenty classical solo titles, and two instructional titles are available. The list is growing rapidly.—ES

Tape Recorders

Create your own Pick-a-track accompaniments. You will need a cassette tape recorder that will allow you to tape to separate tracks one at a time or simultaneously. If simultaneously, one signal can be a line signal, entered directly from an electronic keyboard or other source, and the other a microphone signal from the soloist or solo instrument. Record the line signal only on the left track and the microphone signal only on the right channel. When you play back your recording you can use your balance setting to determine the amount of melody and the amount of accompaniment. Students can use these tapes as practice tools for learning music. More and more, this sort of material is becoming commonly available for purchase. Music educators will have to decide for themselves if such an approach is educationally valid.—BJ; CGB

* * *

A four-track tape recorder can combine with electronic keyboards to be a real teaching and performance tool. If you use prerecorded accompaniment produced by you or your students, that part can be recorded on one track. Special supporting tracks for the singers can be recorded on two other tracks, and the sounds can be sent in such a way that the director (and audience if this is a performance) can hear a balance of accompaniment and singers while the singers hear the supporting parts. As performances near, the supporting materials can be phased out, and finally dropped. Then extra free tracks on the tape machine can be used to record the performance while simultaneously playing the accompaniment. In a similar way, students can use the machine to sing with an accompaniment and then compare their performance with a previously recorded model performance in an extension of the Music Minus One idea.—CGB

Lesson Ideas and Organization

Technology in Classroom and Lab

Organize a class in three-week segments with five students at a time on a keyboard and others doing other things. This takes less equipment and promotes cooperative learning among students.—BJ

* * *

Specialized software may be used to create music crossword puzzles. For example, a crossword puzzle can be based on a film, a video, or a class presentation just seen.—EB

* * *

Carts make it easy to move equipment and are often overlooked in planning equipment purchases.—BJ

* * *

Though much computer/music software is easy to learn, it will not work well if you just turn the students loose with it. You must still plan how the materials fit into the curriculum and precisely how the software is to be used. Part of the lesson plan should be an in-class, "how to" demonstration of the software.—EB

* * *

Class participation is possible, even with a single computer, if you require that no response be made to a question asked by the software until the class agrees what answer is required. This encourages students to discover reasons for their responses, and also trains the entire group in the operation of the program.—PA

* * *

Develop "cheat sheets" that contain all of the various key presses you might need for doing the lesson that uses a computer program. This can be particularly useful when the program is complex (for example, a sequencer program) and you plan to introduce it to students one section at a time.—BJ

* * *

I developed an approach to teaching the compositional elements of music to youngsters (upper elementary and older) using an electronic keyboard bought from Sears for less than $300. The keyboard has MIDI in, out, and thru ports, so it can be connected to all kinds of sound enhancers and computer hardware and software. There are a number of things it can't do or do as well as a more expensive unit, but it does allow the user to pick from about one hundred preset rhythms and an equal number of preset timbres, provide five tracks on which to record and play back melodies, and use effects such as vibrato and portamento to be added to the melodies.

The lesson I developed uses an African folk tune, "Everybody Loves Saturday Night," that can be played as a round and goes well with a Latin-jazz background. In the lesson, students first sing the song, then add an accompaniment on resonator bells using the chords C6 and G9 (the progression consists of alternating measures of each chord). I supply additional accompaniment and rhythm at the piano. I use a handout and discussion to explain the chords, the bass line, and the rhythm of the bass line (a half note and two quarter notes). Ultimately, the students record the bass line on track one, the notes E and F (with rhythmic improvisation) on alternating measures of track two, the note A (or, as a variation, the notes G, G#, A) on track three, the melody on track four, and the melody displaced to form a round on track five of the computer's sequencer program. We can then add preset or newly created percussion rhythm and select timbres and effects for each track. The lesson can be extended into a sequence of lessons by experimenting further with the original tune, selecting other tunes to arrange, creating original pieces, and ultimately extending the instrumental timbres by recording the results on sequencers or playing other sound sources by using MIDI connections.

Plan every detail to be sure that the procedures for recording are understood by the students and to be sure that all contingencies are anticipated. To test the students, ask questions such as: What are the pitches in the C6 (or G9) chord? Which timbres were used on each of the five tracks? What word was used for the slide effect added to the melody? You might also ask them to select the correct line from four variations on the rhythm of the bass line. Using the conventional list of musical elements (including rhythm, pitch, harmony, dynamics, tempo, timbre, texture, form, and style), you can generate many other questions about the structure of the music and the way in which the technology affects the musical structure. In general, the key issue is to use the exercise to emphasize musical concepts rather than simple factual recall.

Even without peripheral devices, the inexpensive electronic keyboard gives you an opportunity to include acoustic and technological concepts such as frequency, attack/decay, envelope, looping, and many others in your teaching.—RP

Computers in Classroom and Lab

Students, at least initially, cannot be turned loose to use computer-based instructional materials without some kind of guidance from teachers. This is especially true of those lessons that provide numerous options for student use, such as drill programs, melodic dictation programs, or harmonic dictation software in which the students can select the items heard and the number of hearings. It is most effective for the teacher to spend some initial time at the computer terminal, demonstrating how to set up the options. Alternately, in a classroom with a large monitor, you can demonstrate how the students can use the program's options. Students can be surprisingly unimaginative in their first use of computer-based technology, and some tend to be "technophobes." A little time spent with the students early on generally helps to defuse objections to the technology, and greatly enhances student learning.—GW

* * *

If you use a general-purpose computer lab, sign up early for lab time. If you do not do so, you may never get to the lab at all. Most lab time is currently being used for word processing or for math drill and practice, and the lab may be fully scheduled early in the year.—EB

* * *

If you find that computers fascinate you, learn about the programs your fellow educators are trying to use, and be helpful. It may pay back in easier access to equipment for your students.—BJ

* * *

Take one practice room and equip it as an electronic music lab! A computer with MIDI interface and sequencing software and a stereo can open up a whole new world to some of your students, especially those interested in composing and recording their own music.—BJ; CW

* * *

Often you can scrounge older computers (Commodore 64s or Apple II+ models, for example) that are not sufficient for use in the computer labs but will work very well with a variety of music software. Install those machines in your room and rotate students to them using theory and ear training software. You will see significant improvement in the students' musical skills.—BJ; CW

* * *

In my music classes (keyboard, voice, and organ), I introduce the computer by the third lesson. In doing so, I give my students an overview of what is available in various software for rudiments, ear training, and simple theory, and I give them guidance about the proper order in which to study the subject matter. The entire class participates with the program by having one student at the computer and others helping to get the correct answers. The correct answer is not entered until the class agrees what answer is required.—PA

Managing Computer Use

- Use small cue cards and tape them in a conspicuous place by the monitor to help students answer questions necessary to get a program to run, such as what options you want them to choose when there are choices.
- Identify the objectives of the software you plan to use when you place it within your current curriculum. Make sure your students know what the objectives are.
- When introducing software that you want each student to use, introduce it by using a liquid crystal display or a large TV or monitor in a class setting and work through the program with the class. Point out places where they may have a problem, such as when their scores appear. (Quite often, unfortunately, students' scores are on a timed screen, which disappears quickly.)
- Primary- and intermediate-age children can be easily frustrated with the computer keyboard, especially if typing skills are necessary to respond to inputs required in software. Clear plastic keyboard overlays that mark the keys used within a program with dots (and that have clues or the purpose of the key written on them) can easily isolate these keys for students. If overlays are not available, have a copy of the keyboard above the computer keyboard with the necessary keys needed to run a program marked clearly with highlight pens or dots.
- Devise effective score- or record-keeping sheets.
- Use a system in which one student works with the program while a second student keeps score for the computer operator. As the second student keeps score, he or she can also see what to do when it is his or her turn to be the operator.—JC
- *Always remember: The computer will do exactly what you tell it to do!*

Appendix: Sources of Information

Note: Only the most common and least expensive sources are listed here. More extensive source lists can be found in many of these sources. Particularly useful are the *ATMI Courseware Directory* and the bibliography of videodisc information in the Spring 1989 issue of *Mus-Disc News.* Since prices are subject to change, check with individual publishers before sending money.

Those interested in electronic instruments will want to contact the major producers of the equipment. All of them produce advertising materials, and most of them produce educational materials they sell or provide free. Some will even do seminars on MIDI and how to use it.

Music and Technology

Alfred Publishing Company. 16380 Roscoe Boulevard, PO Box 10003, Van Nuys, CA 91410-0003. A publisher of materials for computer-based instruction in music.

ATMI Courseware Directory. The Association for Technology in Music Instruction, c/o Dr. Ann Blombach, Music Department, Ohio State University, 110 Wiegel Hall, 1866 College Street, Columbus, OH 43210. Yearly; $15.00 includes quarterly newsletter. An extensive listing of available music software, hardware, and other information related to using technology in music teaching. Updated yearly and available with membership in the Association for Technology in Music Instruction.

CODA Music Software. 1401 E. 79th Street, Minneapolis, MN 55420. One of the major publishers of materials for computer-based instruction in music.

Computers and Music. 1989 Juipero Serra Boulevard, Daly City, CA 94014. Quarterly; approximately $20.00 per year. This quarterly catalog/journal/review booklet published by a leading retailer of computer and electronic music equipment. Strong, reasoned reviews complete with healthy and clearly stated biases.

Contemporary Keyboard Magazine. GPI Corporation, 20085 Stevens Creek, Cupertino, CA 95014, telephone 408-446-7705. Monthly; $23.95 per year. Continuing coverage of electronic music and equipment; materials on keyboard skills and performance.

Electronic Courseware Systems. 1210 Lancaster Drive, Champaign, IL 61821. One of the major publishers of materials for computer-based instruction in music.

Electronic Learning. Scholastic Inc., 730 Broadway, New York, NY 10003-9538. Eight issues per year; 23.95 per year.

Electronic Musician. PO Box 3747, Escondido, CA 92025, telephone

800-334-8152. Monthly; $22.00 per year. Continuing coverage of electronic music and equipment. Somewhat more technically oriented than *Contemporary Keyboard*.

International MIDI Association. 5316 W. Fifty-seventh Street, Los Angeles, CA 90056. *The* source for current information on MIDI specifications. Highly technical and very complete information.

Micro Music. 1535 121st Street, Bellevue, WA 98005. One of the major publishers of materials for computer-based instruction in music.

Mix Bookshelf. 2608 Ninth Street, Berkeley, CA 94710, telephone 800-233-9640. A major seller of books and other materials devoted to all aspects of the electronic music scene. Videotape instruction materials are also available. They appear to handle all known materials from all publishers.

Videodisc, CD, and CDROM

Note: Most of these materials are taken from a more extensive bibliography in *MusDisc News* Volume 1 No. 2 and are used by permission of the editor and the author.—ES; LP

Catalog. Optical Data Corporation, 66 Hanover Road, Box 97, Florham Park, NJ 07932, telephone 201-377-0302.

Catalog. Videodiscovery, PO Box 85878, Seattle, WA 98145-1878, telephone 800-548-3472.

Catalog. Voyager Company, 2139 Manning Avenue, Los Angeles, CA 90025, telephone 213-474-0032.

Catalog. Ztek Company, PO Box 1968, Lexington, KY 40593, telephone 800-247-1603.

CD-ROM End User. DDRI, 6609 Rosecroft Place, Falls Church, VA 22043-1828, telephone 703-241-2131. Monthly; free.

Disc Topics. Pioneer Communications of America, 600 East Crescent Avenue, Upper Saddle River, NJ 07458-1827, telephone 800-527-3766. Quarterly; free.

The Laser Beam. Starship Audio-Industries, 605 Utterback Store Road, Great Falls, VA 22066, telephone 703-430-8692. Free.

The Laser Disc Gazette. RD 2, Box 654, Harpers Ferry, WV 25425. Monthly; free.

The Laser Disc Newsletter. Suite 428, 496A Hudson Street, New York, NY 10014, telephone 212-242-3324. Monthly; $15.00 per year, $2.00 per single issue.

MusDisc News. University of Delaware, Department of Music, Newark, DE 19716, telephone 302-451-2577. Three issues per year; $5.00 per year. This publication is devoted to using audio and video laser discs in teaching music. It is a fine source for keeping up with the field.

Videodisc Design/Production Group News, KUON-TV/University of Nebraska–Lincoln, PO Box 83111, Lincoln, NE 68501-3111, telephone 402-472-3611. Bimonthly; free.

The Videodisc Compendium. Emerging Technology Consultants, PO Box 12444, St. Paul, MN 55112, telephone 612-639-3973. Directory; $8.50.
The Videodisc Monitor. PO Box 26, Falls Church, VA 22046, telephone 800-323-3472. Monthly; $25.00 per year.
Videodiscs for Education: A Directory. Minnesota Educational Computing Corporation, 3490 Lexington Avenue North, St. Paul, MN 55126-8097, telephone 612-481-3500. Third edition, 1988. $10.00.

Database, Spreadsheet, and Word Processing

Rathje, Linda. Appleworks for Educators, International Council for Computers in Education, University of Oregon, 1787 Agate Street, Eugene, OR 97403-1923. Though targeted at the Appleworks user, this volume contains many helpful hints that are applicable to all educators using any multipurpose combination database, spreadsheet, word processor, and/or any combination of such programs that can share data.—JKW

LOGO

Bamberger, Jeanne. "Learning to Think Musically." *Music Educators Journal* 59, no. 7 (March 1973), 53–57.
Papert, Seymour. *Mindstorms: Children, Computers, and Powerful Ideas.* New York: Basic Books, 1980.
Terrapin Music LOGO. Malden, MA: Terrapin, 1986.
Williams, J. Kent. "Talking Music Theory with a Computer and Human Being." *Journal of Computer-Based Instruction* 16, no. 2 (1989, in press).

Acknowledgments

MENC is grateful to the contributors for this book. Their collective knowledge as educators, programmers, writers, and innovative workers in the music industry is a benefit to us all, and we thank them for it. All of the contributors have been active in the Association for Technology in Music Instruction (ATMI), and have been active in giving workshops, lectures, and other presentations dealing with using technology in music instruction.

BJ. Butch Johnson, elementary school teacher, Hopkins Public Schools, Hopkins, MN; owner and operator of a music software and hardware business.

CW. Chip Williams, teacher, Wayzata High School, Wayzata, MN; director of a program that has included electronic music courses for twenty years.

CGB. **Charles G. Boody, compiler,** system analyst/programmer, Hopkins Public Schools, Hopkins, MN; has taught music in public schools and in college; has been active in using computers in music since 1968; immediate past president of ATMI; editor, *ATMI Courseware Directory*.

DBW. David B. Williams, Office of Research in Arts Technology, Illinois State University, Normal, IL; founder of one of the largest producers of software for music education.

EB. Eve Benson, music specialist, Bemidji Public Schools, Bemidji, MN; active in the use of the computer in the elementary school.

ES. Ed Schwartz, instructor, Learning Resources Center, Virginia Polytechnic Institute and State University, Blacksburg, VA; involved in the production of the University of Delaware Music Video Discs.

GT. Gayla Turk, assistant professor, Atlantic Christian College, Wilson, NC; active in music and computing for more than ten years.

GW. Gary Whitlich, professor, Indiana University, Bloomington; a founding member of ATMI; on the editorial board for the University of Delaware Music Video Disc project; software designer.

JB. Judith Bowman, assistant professor, Duquesne University, Pittsburgh, PA; developer of music software.

JC. Juanita Crawford, elementary music specialist, Newark Public Schools, Newark, DE; workshop leader.

JKW. J. Kent Williams, associate professor, University of North

Carolina, Greensboro (involved in using technology to expand learning through creative experiences).

KC. Kate Covington, assistant professor, University of Kentucky, Lexington; software developer; editor of research articles for ATMI.

LP. Larry W. Peterson, associate professor, University of Delaware, Newark; a developer of the University of Delaware Music Video Disc series; founder and editor of *MusDisc News*.

MA. Michael Arenson, associate professor, University of Delaware, Newark; a founding member of ATMI; courseware developer.

PA. Pearl Anshell, independent voice and keyboard teacher, El Cajon, CA; coordinator of two nationwide conferences on the microcomputer in music education.

RJ. Richard Jacobs, professor, University of Maine, Orono; long involved in teaching based on video discs and compact discs.

RP. Robert Placek, professor, University of Georgia, Athens; a founding member of ATMI and author of many software reviews for the *Music Educators Journal*.

TK. J. Timothy Kolosick, associate professor, University of Arizona, Tucson; author of software; director of workshops in music and computing.

TR. Tom Rudolph, instrumental music teacher, Haverford Township High School, Haverford, PA; author and workshop leader.

1096-09-2M-11/92